Minnesota

BY AMY VAN ZEE

The Child's World

Published by The Child's World®
1980 Lookout Drive • Mankato, MN 56003-1705
800-599-READ • www.childsworld.com

ACKNOWLEDGMENTS
The Child's World®: Mary Berendes, Publishing Director
The Design Lab: Design and production
Red Line Editorial: Editorial direction

PHOTO CREDITS: Carol Heesen/Shutterstock Images, cover, 1, 3; Matt
Kania/Map Hero, Inc., 4, 5; Aliaksandr Nikitsin/iStockphoto, 7; Devin
Koob/Shutterstock Images, 9; iStockphoto, 10; Big Stock Photo, 11; Jeffrey
Thompson/AP Images, 13; North Wind Picture Archives/Photolibrary, 15;
Nicole Waring/iStockphoto, 17; Ben Margot/AP Images, 19; AP Images, 21;
One Mile Up, 22; Quarter-dollar coin image from the United States Mint, 22

LIBRARY OF CONGRESS CATALOGING-IN-PUBLICATION DATA
Van Zee, Amy.
 Minnesota / by Amy Van Zee.
   p. cm.
 Includes bibliographical references and index.
 ISBN 978-1-60253-467-4 (library bound : alk. paper)
 1. Minnesota—Juvenile literature. I. Title.

 F606.3.V37 2010
 977.6—dc22

                    2010017719

Printed in the United States of America in Mankato, Minnesota.
July 2010
F11538

On the cover:
There are many
lakes in Voyageurs
National Park
in northern
Minnesota.

CONTENTS

Geography

Let's explore Minnesota! Minnesota is in the north-central United States. This area is called the Midwest. Minnesota shares its northern border with Canada.

CANADA

CANADA

NORTH
DAKOTA

International Falls •
Voyageurs
National
Park

Thief River
Falls •

Grand Portage •

Bemidji •

• Grand Rapids

Lake Superior

Moorhead •

Duluth •

Mississippi River

MICHIGAN

Brainerd •

MINNESOTA

St. Cloud •

Elk River •

SOUTH
DAKOTA

Minneapolis • ★ Saint Paul

WISCONSIN

New Ulm •

Mississippi River

• Pipestone

Rochester •

NORTH

WEST · EAST

Austin •

SOUTH

IOWA

5

Cities

St. Paul is the capital of Minnesota.
Minneapolis is the largest city in the state.
These two cities are called the Twin Cities.
Duluth and Rochester are other large cities
in Minnesota.

Downtown Minneapolis overlooks Lake Calhoun. ▶

Land

About half of the land in Minnesota is farmland. Minnesota also has more than 10,000 lakes. The Mississippi River begins in Minnesota.

Minnesota is called "the Land of 10,000 Lakes."

Northern Minnesota has many lakes and forests. ▶

Plants and Animals

Minnesota has many forests. Many different types of trees grow here. The state tree is the red pine. Its **bark** is reddish-brown. Its leaves are sharp like needles. The state flower is the lady's-slipper. It is pink and white. The loon is the state bird. Loons are water birds that swim and dive well.

A lady's-slipper grows 12 to 24 inches (30–61 cm) tall. ▶

People and Work

More than 5 million people live in Minnesota. Farming is the largest **industry** in this state. Other important industries are logging, mining, and fishing. People in Minnesota work in **manufacturing**, too. They make **chemicals** and **equipment**.

A farmer works on his field in southern Minnesota. ▶

History

People from Europe first came to Minnesota in the 1600s. They were fur traders. When they arrived, they found many Native Americans living on the land. In 1849, the Minnesota **Territory** was created. It was much larger than the state of Minnesota is today. Minnesota became the thirty-second state on May 11, 1858.

Fur traders sometimes caught beavers in traps. ▶

Ways of Life

With so many lakes, Minnesota offers a lot of outdoor activities. In the summer, people enjoy boating and swimming. There are trails for jogging, biking, and **hiking**. Many people in Minnesota like to hunt and fish. Minnesota has very cold winters. Many people enjoy ice skating, hockey, and skiing.

In Minnesota, hockey can be played on ▶ frozen lakes and ponds in the winter.

Famous People

Cartoonist Charles Schulz was born and raised in Minnesota. He drew characters such as Snoopy and Charlie Brown. Writers Sinclair Lewis and F. Scott Fitzgerald and singer Judy Garland were from Minnesota. Former U.S. Vice President Walter Mondale is also from the state.

Charles Schulz first drew the comic strip "Peanuts" in 1950. ▶

Famous Places

Many people who visit Minnesota like to go to the Mall of America. It is the largest shopping mall in the United States. The Mall of America has a theme park inside it called Nickelodeon Universe. Visitors here enjoy the rides and games. The Mayo Clinic is also in Minnesota. This famous **medical** center is known for its **research**.

The Mall of America has more than 400 stores. ▶

The Mall of America is the size of 78 football fields put together.

State Symbols

Seal

The Minnesota state seal shows a man plowing. This stands for Minnesota's farming. Go to childsworld.com/links for a link to Minnesota's state Web site, where you can get a firsthand look at the state seal.

Flag

The flag has the seal on it. The stump on the seal stands for logging in the state.

Quarter

A loon and a fisherman are on the Minnesota state quarter. It came out in 2005.

Glossary

bark (BARK): Bark is the covering on a tree trunk. The bark on the red pine, Minnesota's state tree, is reddish brown.

chemicals (KEM-uh-kulz): Chemicals are substances used in chemistry. Some people in Minnesota make chemicals.

equipment (ih-KWIP-munt): Equipment is the set of items needed to do something. Some people in Minnesota make equipment.

hiking (HYK-ing): Hiking is taking a walk in a natural area, such as a hill or a mountain. People in Minnesota enjoy hiking.

industry (IN-duh-stree): Industry is factories and other companies that make things. Farming is a large industry in Minnesota.

manufacturing (man-yuh-FAK-chur-ing): Manufacturing is the task of making items with machines. People who work in manufacturing in Minnesota make chemicals and equipment.

medical (MED-uh-kul): Medical is some-thing that relates to medicine. The Mayo Clinic in Minnesota is a medical center.

plowing (PLOW-ing): Plowing is turning over soil before planting seeds. The Minnesota state seal shows a man plowing his land.

research (REE-surch): Research is studying or experimenting on something. The Mayo Clinic in Minnesota is well known for its research.

seal (SEEL): A seal is a symbol a state uses for government business. The farmer on the Minnesota state seal stands for the state's farming.

symbols (SIM-bulz): Symbols are pictures or things that stand for something else. The seal and the flag are Minnesota's symbols.

territory (TAYR-uh-tor-ee): A territory is a piece of land that is controlled by another country. Minnesota was part of the Minnesota Territory before becoming a state.

Further Information

Books

Davis, Kenneth C. *The Fifty States*. New York: HarperCollins Publishers, 2001.

Heinrichs, Ann. *Minnesota*. Mankato, MN: Child's World, 2006.

Wargin, Kathy-jo. *V is for Viking: A Minnesota Alphabet*. Chelsea, MI: Sleeping Bear Press, 2003.

Web Sites

Visit our Web site for links about Minnesota: *childsworld.com/links*

Note to Parents, Teachers, and Librarians: We routinely verify our Web links to make sure they are safe and active sites. So encourage your readers to check them out!

Index